PPA GUIDELIN

GOOD PRACTICE FOR PARENT AND TODDLER PLAYGROUPS

CONTENTS

APPENDICES

Wherever the word **"parent"** is used in these guidelines, it should be taken to mean **"parent or carer"**, as parents are not necessarily the only adults who care for and have responsibility for young children.

ACKNOWLEDGEMENTS

This set of guidelines was compiled by members of PPA at all levels. Special thanks go to the Code of Practice Group and the Daycare Development Group and to all those volunteers and staff who contributed to the development of this publication.

Cover photograph: Margaret Hanton

PPA GUIDELINES

GOOD PRACTICE FOR PARENT AND TODDLER PLAYGROUPS

INTRODUCTION

Over the last 29 years, parents in every part of the country have set up playgroups to provide care and education for their pre-school children. Most of these playgroups are members of PPA and have benefitted from its advice, support and training.

Groups where parents meet for companionship and mutual support whilst their babies and toddlers enjoy a variety of play opportunities have also flourished. These groups, many of which were originally called mother and toddler clubs, have similarly become part of the PPA network.

This publication, **Good Practice for Parent and Toddler Playgroups**, is for all such groups. It complements two other PPA Guidelines: *Good Practice for Sessional Playgroups* and *Good Practice for Full Daycare Playgroups*.

All three publications have been written in response to requests from PPA members who are anxious to ensure that their groups make the best possible provision for children and parents. They draw together the advice, policy and good practice that have been developed and recommended over a number of years through articles in *Contact* magazine, through the work of PPA's national committees, in AGM resolutions and in PPA publications. They cover the joint thinking of groups in all parts of the country as expressed through the Association's democratic network of fieldwork support.

DEFINITIONS

PPA uses the following definitions:

● **Parent and toddler playgroup** – a group of parents or carers with children under school age, most of the children below the age of three. These groups provide for both children and adults. Parents remain with the child(ren) throughout the session.

● **Mother and baby group** – a group set up to provide post-natal support for mothers and their babies. The children in the group are usually under a year old.

1

- **Family drop-in centre** – a group that offers opportunities for families to attend sessions, as and when they wish, with children of any age. Family drop-in centres often provide specific advice and counselling sessions for parents.

- **Under-fives playgroup** – a group offering sessional care for children mainly aged three to five years of age cared for with or without their parents. Children under this age also attend with a responsible adult who remains throughout the session. No session lasts for more than four hours (ie a playgroup and a parent and toddler playgroup running a combined session).

- **Playgroup** – a group offering sessional care for children mainly aged three to five years of age cared for with or without parents, no session lasting more than 4 hours. A few call themselves "nursery", although they are registered as playgroups.

- **Opportunity playgroup** – a group that is set up primarily to provide for children with disabilities or learning difficulties alongside other children. The children often start at an earlier age than in a regular playgroup and staff usually have more specialised training in this field.

- **Full daycare playgroup** – a group that accepts children under the age of five, without their parents, for more than four hours in any day.

Many different names are used by groups which PPA defines as parent and toddler playgroups, eg mums and tots, parent and young club, bumps and lumps, pram and pushchair group, one o'clock club.

There are a great many other variations and combinations of groups which cater for the under-five-year-old, including groups run in hospital clinics and on wards, in playbuses and creches in shopping centres, sports centres, colleges etc.

These Guidelines are written primarily for parent and toddler playgroups but apply also to other groups where parents remain responsible for their own children. The term "group" has been used throughout to refer to all such groups. Occasionally comments refer specifically to a particular kind of group, such as a mother and baby group or family drop-in centre.

Playgroups which care for children in the absence of their parents or carers, whether or not they have a legal requirement to register with the local social services department, should refer to PPA's *Good Practice for Sessional Playgroups* or, if children are accepted for more than four hours in any day, PPA's *Good Practice for Full Daycare Playgroups*.

Under-fives playgroups should go through the proper registration procedure and follow the recommendations set out in *Good Practice for Sessional Playgroups* as well as considering the needs of younger children and their parents set out in these Guidelines.

PPA recognises the variations that exist, and should exist, when parents set up groups to meet their own needs and those of the local community.

PPA believes that, although there are many differences – in the way groups run, their size and type of premises, the emphasis which they place upon support for parents and play for children, and even in the age range of the children they cater for – **the basic principles for good practice remain the same.**

Groups which do not have to register with social services, since parents remain responsible for their own children, are responsible for setting and maintaining their own standards for the happiness, welfare and safety of all their members.

Groups will be able to use this publication to help define their own goals and identify areas where they need to make changes. They should interpret the more detailed guidance in the booklet in a way that is appropriate to their own situation.

The Guidelines should also help when requesting grant aid or pointing out the needs of the group – such as for messy play activities or chairs which can be stacked safely – to a reluctant landlord.

PPA believes that by following these basic principles, and implementing as much as possible of these guidelines in the way that is most appropriate for them, groups will ensure a happy, supportive environment for parents and a stimulating, worthwhile experience for children.

PRINCIPLES

PPA believes that:

There should be opportunities in every locality for parents with babies and toddlers to meet together.

Groups should identify and respond to the needs of the local community and the changing needs of members.

Groups should aim to create a warm, friendly atmosphere where newcomers are welcomed and can soon become part of the group.

Parents are the main educators of their children; the informal learning about parenting and the support for parents which take place in groups should be recognised and promoted.

Groups should welcome and provide for children and adults with disabilities and learning difficulties.

Group premises should be safe, suitable and easily accessible.

Groups should be of a manageable size and children should be well supervised.

Opening times should be convenient for local families.

Groups should have clear policies and sound management procedures; parents should be involved in all aspects of the group including management.

The session should be organised to meet the needs of both adults and children.

Groups should provide good quality, safe, educational play, with equipment and activities appropriate to the children's ages and stages of development.

Groups should ensure that any food or drink provided is prepared hygienically, served safely and appropriate to the needs of adults and children.

Groups should have appropriate and adequate insurance cover.

All groups should pay realistic expenses to volunteers; groups employing staff should comply with all employment legislation and pay adequate salaries.

Volunteers and staff in groups need to develop attitudes and skills which promote the self-esteem and well-being of both adults and children.

Groups should maintain close links with other local provision and services for under-fives and their families.

Groups in all areas should promote equal opportunities and should reflect the multi-cultural nature of our society in their equipment and activities.

OPPORTUNITIES TO MEET

There should be opportunities in every locality for parents with babies and toddlers to meet together

in order to

foster mutual support for parents, reduce social isolation and provide play opportunities for children.

1 Parents should be encouraged to understand and provide for their own needs and those of their children. This can be done through community groups where parents can meet together with their small children.

2 Groups where parents remain responsible for their own children throughout the session do not need to register with the local social services department.

3 Groups should be open and welcoming to all adults who are, or soon will be, responsible for the care of small children except where the group has been set up to cater for specific sections of the community, eg women's refuges, or where religious or cultural beliefs might prevent women from attending if men were present.

4 Parents of small children need opportunities to meet regardless of the ages of their children. Groups should consider how this can be best achieved in their own locality.
- Most groups cater for all children from birth to at least age three.
- Some groups have separate mother and baby sections.
- Some groups have extra sessions with extended play opportunities for over-twos accompanied by their parents.
- Many groups include children up to school age and even beyond.

Policies on moving from one section to another should be openly discussed and agreed.

⑤ Wherever possible, families should be able to remain in the group after their child reaches the age of three. This is particularly important when
- there is a younger child in the family who would otherwise be unable to attend;
- the parent still needs support from the group;
- a playgroup place is not available for the child.

⑥ There should be recognition of the value of groups for parents and small children and appropriate funding for their development.

⑦ There should be a co-ordinated national policy for under-fives which involves PPA in the planning, development, support and training of groups locally and nationally. Such support should recognise the individuality of each group and acknowledge that they may open and close as needs change.

IDENTIFYING THE NEEDS

Groups should identify and respond to the needs of the local community and the changing needs of members

in order to

ensure that all families have access to the type of group which best suits their needs.

[1] Before starting a group it is important to find out whether there is a need, determine what type of group will fulfil it and then plan accordingly. Groups may start up informally, with a few parents meeting together in each other's homes, and possibly look for alternative premises at a later date.

[2] The research can be done in several ways:
- consultation with local parents
- via local clinics, health visitors and mother and baby groups
- at local playgroups and schools
- notices in local shops and community buildings
- consultation with PPA
- consultation with local community associations, community relations councils and councils for racial equality
- surveys and public meetings.

[3] As well as consulting with mothers, consideration should be given to the particular needs of pregnant women, fathers, childminders, foster parents, nannies, grandparents and any other adults responsible for the care of babies and toddlers.

[4] Once the group is established, it should continue to consider and respond to the needs of its members as the group changes in size, composition or the ages of the children.

[5] Groups should maintain good relationships with health visitors and local community leaders. This will help to identify the needs of those not

currently attending the group and sections of the community who may be under-represented, eg ethnic minority groups, lone parents, first time mothers or children and adults with disabilities.

EQUAL OPPORTUNITIES CONSIDERATIONS

i   Parents from ethnic minority communities should be encouraged to identify their own particular needs. Groups initiated by ethnic minority parents, organisations and communities should be actively supported by the PPA network.

ii   Groups aiming to meet the needs of homeless families and other families facing disadvantage should work in partnership with local voluntary agencies and professionals to make the best use of community resources.

PROVIDING A WELCOME

Groups should aim to create a warm, friendly atmosphere where newcomers are welcomed and can soon become part of the group

in order to

encourage parents and children to relax and enjoy time spent together in the company of other adults and children.

1 Groups should ensure that everyone who comes to the group is greeted in a warm friendly manner. A person or group of people should be given the responsibilty for seeing that this welcome is maintained.

2 Newcomers should be introduced to other parents, particularly those who live near them or have a child of a similar age, to ensure that nobody is ignored or left isolated. Cliques should be actively discouraged. The adults responsible for running the group need to be aware that they are leading by example.

3 Adults should be encouraged to talk to everyone within the group and assured that formal introductions are unnecessary.

4 A brief explanation about how the group is run should be given to each parent. Verbal information could be backed up by a welcome letter or leaflet giving the following information:
- days and times of opening (including holiday periods)
- name and phone number of a contact person
- how much the group charges
- what happens at the session
- how each child remains the responsibility of the parent/carer
- who is responsible for running the group
- in what ways parents are expected to help
- any 'rules' of the group, including those about safety and behaviour.

5 Groups should consider if their name appears to be restrictive in any way (eg *Mother & Toddler* could be taken to mean no fathers or childminders

and no babies). Except where a group is set up to provide for a specific section of the community, any advertising should show that the group is open to all who care for small children.

6 Groups should advertise as widely as possible throughout the local community, and not just rely on word of mouth, in order to make themselves known to all parents including those who may be particularly isolated through having just moved to the area or given up paid employment.

7 Suitable places for advertising include local shops, especially newsagents, toy shops and chemists; post offices; doctors' surgeries, ante-natal clinics; baby clinics; libraries; churches, mosques, temples and other places where cultural or religious activities take place; school and community newsletters; local papers; council offices; estate agents; playgroups and community buildings.

8 If groups have a regular meeting place they should advertise clear details of meeting days and times, with a contact name, both inside and, if possible, outside the building.

9 The entrance and directions to the meeting place should be indicated.

10 Groups which meet in a different place each week should ensure that contact names are well-publicised and regularly updated so that new members can get in touch with the group.

11 Groups which meet in each other's homes should not exclude parents who feel unable, for whatever reason, to take a turn as hosts.

12 Groups should try to identify parents who need a companion or a lift for the first few sessions or other extra support to encourage them to join the group. Health visitors, social services departments, Home Start schemes and National Childbirth Trust groups may know of such families.

EQUAL OPPORTUNITIES CONSIDERATIONS

i   Groups should reflect the multi-cultural nature of society in order to be welcoming to all sections of the community.

ii   Groups should advertise and have information about the group available in languages appropriate to the needs of the local community, and try to learn some words of welcome in these languages.

iii   Groups should use terms like 'first name' and 'family name' – not 'Christian name'. They should ensure that names are written correctly and pronounced accurately, and that it is clear what name the child or adult wishes to be called, since the order of words may vary.

iv   Groups which use the term 'mother and toddler playgroup' should consider whether it would be more appropriate to change the name to 'parent and toddler playgroup'.

SAFETY CONSIDERATIONS

i   An accurate register of all adults and children should be kept throughout the session. This should be filled in as parents arrive and leave in case of a fire or other emergency.

SUPPORT FOR PARENTS

Parents are the main educators of their children; the informal learning about parenting and the support for parents which take place in groups should be recognised and promoted

in order to

increase parents' confidence in themselves and their role, reduce stress and foster a greater understanding of the needs of children.

[1] Those involved in running or supporting groups should recognise the importance of the informal learning about parenting and the support for parents which take place there.

[2] Parents should be encouraged to share experiences, joys and concerns in a non-judgmental, relaxed atmosphere. Someone whose child has either just been through or is going through a similar stage of development can be an invaluable source of information and support.

[3] The layout of the room should make it easy for adults to talk to one another. This can be accomplished by arranging small groups of chairs around activities. Isolated chairs, huge circles or rows of chairs should be avoided.

[4] Adult-size chairs should be provided so that parents, particularly pregnant or nursing mothers, can sit comfortably.

[5] Groups should provide opportunities for shared play, suitable for the ages and stages of development of the children. By watching their own and other children at play, parents will increase their understanding of child development and gain ideas for suitable activities for their child.

[6] Groups should encourage parents who wish to try out activities at home. This could be done by:
- providing information, eg recipes for dough
- keeping details of stockists of suitable equipment
- demonstrating the use of easily available materials for making

equipment, eg washing-up bottles for non-spill paint pots, boxes for cooker tops, paper bags or socks for puppets

● selling small quantities of cooked dough, paint or other art materials

● loaning books and leaflets.

[7] Whilst all parents should be encouraged to spend time with their children, groups should recognise the needs of parents to relax and talk.

[8] Groups should give consideration to the particular needs of parents who have twins or other multiple births.

[9] Forming baby-sitting circles, arranging social events and outings and selling nearly new clothing and equipment should be considered.

[10] Groups should make information and advice readily available to parents. The ways this could be done include:

● having leaflets and posters from a variety of sources, including PPA, the local health authority and social services

● providing information on other sources of help within the local community

● displaying telephone numbers or addresses of national organisations which provide support for parents (see Appendix)

● arranging for health visitors to visit the group either to talk informally to parents or to hold a regular baby clinic

● arranging for talks, discussions, advice and counselling sessions, workshops or short courses to be held either during the session or in the evening

Parents should be encouraged to identify the information they require and the form it should take.

[11] Some parents need support beyond the capacity of a self-help situation. Groups should encourage parents to seek professional advice and counselling where appropriate.

[12] Groups should ensure that both adults and children receive appropriate attention and support during the session. In order to achieve this, groups may decide to involve extra volunteers or employ staff whose role could include

● welcoming members and making contact with new or shy adults

- supporting parents, including listening to any parent who needs to talk
- keeping an eye on a baby or toddler whilst the parent plays with another child
- playing with the children
- organising equipment, play materials, refreshments and furniture.

13   Groups may also wish to involve volunteers or staff as outreach workers or home visitors. Family drop-in centres should consider employing a paid co-ordinator whose role could also include liaising with other voluntary agencies and professionals. This co-ordinator should aim to develop a full understanding of the cultures of the family drop-in centre users.

14   Groups should ensure that all parents, volunteers and staff have access to PPA and other relevant training opportunities in order to extend the informal learning which take place in the group.

15   Parents, by joining a group which is a National PPA member, automatically join PPA. They should be encouraged to gain full benefit from their membership by participating in branch meetings, training days and other events. They should be asked if they would like to take out a parent subscription to *Contact* and purchase *Under Five* magazine at a discount through the group.

16   Groups should seek financial aid, expertise and resourcing from the relevant local authority departments and have access to support and resource facilities through the PPA network at all levels.

EQUAL OPPORTUNITIES CONSIDERATIONS

i   Groups should encourage respect for different forms of child rearing patterns and practices. The information available in the group should reflect these practices and be in languages appropriate to the needs of the local community.

ii Groups should recognise that some parents for whom English is the second langauge may choose to communicate with each other in their first language.

iii Groups should encourage the building of support networks for parents of children with disabilities and learning difficulties. Integration of families into the community is easiest at this stage before children are separated into more specialised forms of provision.

SAFETY CONSIDERATIONS

i   Children should still be adequately supervised while parents talk or participate in adult activities. Groups which provide additional adult activities or facilities, such as sewing classes or washing machines, should have sufficient volunteers or staff to ensure the safety of the children.

CHILDREN AND ADULTS WITH DISABILITIES OR LEARNING DIFFICULTIES

Groups should welcome and provide for children and adults with disabilities and learning difficulties

in order to

ensure that all members of the community have access to a local group.

1 PPA recognises that 15-20% of children have special educational needs at some time. PPA believes that all children, wherever possible, should have their needs catered for within the community. Groups should provide for children with special needs alongside other children and give help and support to parents.

2 Groups should consider how their premises and facilities could be made more accessible and appropriate for people with disabilities. Groups in rented premises should encourage the owner or hall committee to make any necessary alterations.

3 Groups should try to obtain any appropriate special equipment. There may be a Toy Library available with equipment specifically designed for children with disabilities or toys may be borrowed from the local PPA branch.

4 Children and adults with disabilities or learning difficulties may need assistance with travelling to and from the group. Groups should investigate the provision of lifts or a taxi.

5 Groups should provide for adults with disabilities or learning difficulties as appropriate, eg help with looking after children, an escort or use of sign language.

[6] Groups should discuss with parents any issues which concern them and identify further ways in which the group might be of assistance.

[7] Groups should recognise that caring for a child with disabilities or learning difficulties can be very exhausting and stressful.

[8] Groups should seek appropriate information, training, advice and support from the PPA network or any relevant statutory or voluntary agency.

[9] Adults and children with disabilities or learning difficulties should be included in all group activities wherever possible.

[10] PPA recommends that children and adults with AIDS or who are HIV positive should be included in groups as they pose no risks to others in the group as long as normal hygiene rules are observed. Both children and adults benefit from a reduction in isolation. PPA believes the benefits of attendance for children with AIDS or who are HIV positive far outweigh the risk of picking up ordinary infections. More information can be found in PPA's Information Sheets.

[11] Further information regarding children with special needs is available in *All Children are Special* (PPA publication 1989) and in PPA Information Sheets.

SAFETY CONSIDERATIONS

i Groups should take extra special care about safety for children and adults with disabilities and learning difficulties.

ii Groups should inform parents that their child may not be covered in all circumstances under the personal accident section of the insurance policy but should reassure them that, under the public liability clauses, all children are covered.

PREMISES

Group premises should be safe, suitable and easily accessible

in order to

provide the best possible environment for young children and their families.

General

1 All groups should meet in premises which are suitable for young children and adults and which conform to appropriate safety standards.

2 Groups should do all they can, within the limitations of their finances and the constraints of the premises, to promote the physical comfort and well-being of adults and children.

Home Groups

3 Groups which meet in people's homes should interpret the guidelines for hall based groups in ways which are appropriate to their situation.

Hall Groups

4 PPA recommends groups contact the social services department and/or the local PPA branch for help and support when choosing premises. Planning permission may be necessary. The Fire Officer may give further advice on safety and space required.

5 Groups sharing premises should ensure that the activities of other users are compatible with under fives provision. Unsuitable activities are those likely to cause deterioration of the premises or equipment, to cause damage through misuse or to affect the general running of the group.

6 The premises should be convenient and accessible for local parents and should be in good repair.

7 A covered area should be available to leave prams, pushchairs or buggies. Hanging space should be provided for outdoor clothing.

8 There should be adequate, safe and accessible storage space in which

equipment can be locked away between sessions.

9   The building should be welcoming and friendly with a bright positive atmosphere. Wherever possible, mobiles, posters and children's paintings should be displayed where babies and young children can easily see them.

10   Groups in large halls should structure the environment to give a cosier atmosphere. Carpets, screens, cushions, etc can all be used to reduce noise levels.

11   All groups should have access to a telephone on the premises or close by.

12   Heating and ventilation systems should enable comfortable temperatures to be maintained. The minimum should be 65°F with 70°F preferable for babies.

13   Toilet facilities should be adequate for the number of children involved. Nappy changing facilities and provision for disposable nappies should be available. Any changing mats, potties and trainer seats provided must be regularly disinfected.

14   Wash basins should ideally have thermostatically controlled hot (30°C) and cold running water. Wherever possible toilets and wash basins should be low level, or made accessible by provision of non-slip stools.

15   Individual paper towels should be provided. If hot air hand driers are installed in the building, parents should supervise their use by children.

16   All rooms should be well lit with plenty of natural light. Ideally windows should be low enough for children to see the outside world.

EQUAL OPPORTUNITIES CONSIDERATIONS

i   Ideally there should be at least one unisex toilet for disabled use.

ii   The buildings and any outside playspace should be fully accessible for adults and children with disabilities. (BS 5810 1979 British Standard Code of Practice for the Disabled, Access to Buildings).

ADDITIONAL SAFETY CONSIDERATIONS

Home Groups

i   Groups meeting in different people's homes should help each host to check for safety factors, especially where the ages of the host's children do not cover the range of the whole group. Hosts should remove items which can be damaged or cause accidents, eg glass tables, valuable ornaments.

Hall Groups

ii   Groups renting halls should bring any safety factors regarding the premises to the notice of the owner or hall committee and ensure that action is taken.

iii   Sleeping babies should not be left unattended outside the premises, or out of sight of the group. A suitable space should be found where parents can watch sleeping children.

iv   Groups in shared premises should ensure that other users do not put young children at risk; eg floors should be properly disinfected after dog-training classes, debris removed after hall-lettings, stacks of tables and chairs checked for stability, piano lids secured open or shut.

v   Fire exits should not be locked and access to them must be kept clear at all times. If problems are likely to be experienced with children leaving the building unescorted, the Fire Officer's advice should be sought before fitting any form of locking device. If the main entrance has to be kept locked to ensure safety of children or property, the key must be left in the door or hanging near it in a known safe place and there should be a door bell.

vi   Doors should be fitted with slow closing mechanisms to prevent children's fingers being trapped. Any glass in doors or low windows should be safety glass or protected with a rigid covering. Any internal doors left open during the session should be securely fixed open.

vii   Toilet doors should not be lockable by children.

viii   Stairways should be well-lit and equipped with handrails and stair-gates at the top and bottom as appropriate. Other internal safety gates should be fitted where necessary, for example to prevent access to the kitchen or stage.

ix   Floors should have non-slip surfaces; wooden floors should be devoid of splinters. Baby areas should have easily washable floor coverings. All floors should be kept clean, especially where outside shoes or prams may have brought dirt or animal faeces into the group.

x   The kitchen should be kept clean, hygienic and well ventilated. Safety precautions should be observed at all times.

xi   Heating appliances should be sited in a safe place, serviced regularly and suitably guarded.

xii   Electrical plugs and power points should be protected from children or made inaccessible. Electrical leads should not be loose or trailing and power points should not be overloaded.

xiii   Proper fire precautions should be taken, fire drills regularly practised where appropriate and fire equipment regularly serviced. Written fire instructions should be displayed in each room and by each phone. (Further details may be found in the Appendix.)
Ideally smoke detectors should be fitted and should be checked periodically.

xiv   Curtains and furnishings should be non-flammable and conform to appropriate British Standards.

xv   Groups should either ban smoking on the premises or set aside special areas for adults who smoke. Smoking areas should be clearly labelled and preferably be well away from the children's play area. New groups should consider their policy before opening since a no-smoking policy is much harder to introduce once the group has begun.

xvi Any outdoor play space should be securely fenced and gated, with impact absorbing surfaces in the areas around play structures. Ponds, pools or any natural water should be adequately guarded. If possible there should be some area with shade. The play space should be kept clear of animal faeces and other hazards.

xvii Groups should provide a first aid box and secure storage for all potentially dangerous products.

xviii Dustbins, ash trays and litter bins should not be accessible to children and should be emptied regularly.

xix Arrangements should be made for safe arrival and departure, including car parking.

FURNITURE FOR PARENT AND TODDLER PLAYGROUPS

The amount and type of furniture will depend upon the type and size of the group. Not all groups will need every item of furniture listed. A mother and baby group will concentrate on comfortable seating for mothers and clean, padded flooring for babies. A family drop-in centre may provide extra facilities for parents to prepare meals.

Groups renting premises should establish what is already available for their use. It is helpful to have an outline plan of the building and a clear idea of what storage space is available before obtaining any extra furniture. Large items of furniture are best on castors for ease of movement.

Groups which meet in people's homes will generally use what is available in the home although extra items, eg safety equipment and cleaning materials, may be required solely for the use of the group.

For main hall or playroom:
Chairs and tables, both adult and child-size
Settees or easy chairs, sagbags and/or large cushions
Soft and easily washable padded floor covering (eg foam-filled vinyl, quilted materials) for the baby area

Baby chairs
Carpets, screens, blinds or curtains
Book display cupboard or rack
Adequately guarded heaters
Fire extinguishers
Protective floor covering for messy play area.

In main hall or nearby:
Sink for mixing paints/washing up after messy play
Storage cupboards – preferably including a large lockable walk-in storage area
Coat hooks
Book case
Lockable storage space for cleaning materials.

For the kitchen and food preparation areas
Sinks, draining boards and adult hand washing facilities
Kettle
Crockery and cutlery suitable for adults and children
Storage cupboards for food, cutlery and crockery
Storage containers for food
Ample surfaces for food and drink preparation
Tea-towels and handtowels
Rubbish bin
Fire blanket
If intending to cook – pots, pans and other utensils from appropriate cultures
Cooker, refrigerator, microwave oven and other electrical gadgets if needed.

For the toilets
Paper towels or hand drier machine
Non-slip step-up stools
Trainer seats and potties
Nappy changing facilities including changing mat or trolley
Bucket or bin for disposable nappies
Mirror
Sanitary protection vending machine and disposal unit (probably on a contract basis).

For cleaning and clearing up
Rubbish bins and dustbins
Dustpans and brushes
Brooms, dusters, mops, buckets, disposable cleaning cloths
Assorted cleaning materials
Vacuum cleaner.

Miscellaneous needs
Safety gates
Noticeboard and leaflet rack
Safe storage for information
Telephone
Cash box
First aid box and accident book.

GROUP SIZE AND SUPERVISION

Groups should be of a manageable size and children should be well supervised

in order to

maintain a secure environment from which adults and children can gain maximum benefit.

[1] Groups should consider the size of the premises and the degree of adult involvement with the children when deciding upon maximum numbers. Parents and children need to be able to locate each other quickly in case of an emergency.

[2] Groups which feel they are becoming uncomfortably or dangerously overcrowded should consider opening an extra session, suggesting that parents who come more than once a week attend fewer sessions or finding alternative premises.

[3] Methods of limiting numbers should be discussed openly so that no-one feels they are being unfairly excluded. The Fire Officer's advice about maximum safe numbers must be heeded. Operating age limits and waiting lists or accepting members only from the immediate locality are other, though less desirable, methods of restricting numbers.

[4] Numbers attending groups often fluctuate. Groups should review their policy regularly to ensure they do not impose restrictions unnecessarily.

[5] Parents should be present throughout the session and remain responsible for the children they bring with them. This should be explained clearly to parents when they first come to the group.

[6] Childminders should bring to the group only their own children and those for whom they are legally registered. The maximum is normally three under-fives.

⑦ Groups may agree a policy where, in special circumstances, a parent may make a private arrangement with another individual to take responsibility for her/his child at the group. **Neither the group as a whole, nor an individual on behalf of the group, should accept responsibility for another person's child during the session.**
If a group does allow any such private arrangement to be made, then the number of children any one adult (other than the parent) can be responsible for in the group should not normally exceed three (including her/his own children).

⑧ Parents with large families, however, should be able to bring all their children so long as they are within any age limits set by the group.

⑨ Any extra volunteers and staff who are involved in the group can play an active role in maintaining the level of supervision but should not assume total responsibility for the children. Like every adult in the group, they should be prepared to remove hazards and prevent accidents.

SAFETY CONSIDERATIONS

i No member of staff or volunteer who has not been registered with the social services department (see section on *Employing Staff*) should be expected by the group to take a child or small group of children anywhere on their own, especially into another room or to the toilets.

ii Parents can make their own private arrangements to take each other's children to the toilets or keep an eye on the children whilst one parent is busy. Parents should be aware that it is their own responsibility to ensure that such arrangements are satisfactory.

OPENING TIMES

Opening times should be convenient for local families

in order to

enable them to attend the group.

[1]   Groups should consult regularly with parents about the suitability of their opening times and, if possible, adjust the times accordingly.

[2]   When fixing opening times groups should consider other commitments which parents may have such as taking older children to, and collecting them from, playgroup or school.

[3]   Groups which meet for one or two short sessions each week should consider whether they can open on different days or times from other groups in the area, thus extending the opportunities available to parents. A choice of a morning or afternoon session is valuable to fit in with children's sleeping routines.

[4]   In parent and toddler playgroups, mother and baby groups and family drop-in centres, parents and children should be able to attend all or part of the session. Under-fives playgroups may have a policy whereby the younger children attend for only part of the session.

[5]   Wherever possible, groups should avoid operating waiting lists or insisting that parents lose their place if they do not attend regularly. Families should be able to attend the group as and when they wish.

[6]   Groups such as family drop-in centres which are open for longer hours should ensure that members of staff or volunteers are always present during the time that the centre is advertised as being open.

[7]   Groups should consider whether they will continue to operate during the school holidays.

8   Groups which remain open should decide whether they are able to welcome school age children and should make their policy clear to parents. Some older children might enjoy caring for and playing with their younger siblings; others might need extensive additional provision if the group is to remain safe and enjoyable for its usual members.

9   Groups which close during the school holidays should notify parents clearly about the dates they will be shut.

SAFETY CONSIDERATIONS

i   Groups should pay particular attention to the safety of people arriving early or leaving late in the day. No-one should be expected or asked to be in the building or wait outside it alone at any time.

POLICIES AND MANAGEMENT

Groups should have clear policies and sound management procedures; parents should be involved in all aspects of the group including management

in order to

strengthen and build on parental responsibility; ensure that agreed policies are implemented, that resources are used effectively and that legal aid, where appropriate, constitutional obligations are fulfilled.

[1] Groups can be set up and run in a variety of ways:
- by the parents themselves, as an informal group
- by one or two of the parents
- by an elected committee of parents
- jointly with a sessional playgroup
- by another individual, such as a health visitor
- by a steering committee involving the PPA branch and/or other voluntary or statutory agencies. (This particularly applies to family drop-in centres.)
- by another organisation, such as the local church, school or community association.

Parents should always be made aware of who is responsible for running the group and should be consulted regularly about the style of provision, the play activities for the children and the policies of the group.

[2] PPA recommends that wherever possible the group should be managed by the parents themselves. PPA believes that involvement in the group and its management can help parents make the best use of their own knowledge and resources in the development of their children and themselves.

[3] Groups which meet in people's homes and where no money changes hands – except perhaps to pay for refreshments – could possibly be run in a totally informal way with the whole group taking responsibility for all decisions.

4 Groups which collect money, such as to pay rent or buy toys, need to be clear who is responsible for looking after this money, accounting for it and deciding how it is spent.

5 In larger groups it is more difficult for everyone to be involved in decision-making. Decisions should not be left to one or two people who select themselves. An elected management committee makes it clear where responsibilities lie and gives all parents the opportunity to be involved in running the group.

6 Individuals who take on running a group without a formal election procedure for a management committee should be aware that they could be held personally responsible for any activities of the group (eg insurance claims, financial commitments etc.)

7 PPA recommends groups should have a written set of rules or guidelines which show where the responsibilities lie. These rules should also make clear what the 'aim' of the group is and explain how its assets, eg toys, money and equipment, would be disposed of if the group were to close.

8 PPA has a set of rules called the *PPA Constitution* which groups may adopt. This automatically gives most groups charitable status and means that they can legally raise funds from the public and are eligible to apply for grants.

9 Charitable status can also be gained through adopting their own constitution and getting it approved by the Charity Commissioners or through being an integral part of another charity, such as a church or community association.

10 A set of rules which has been devised and adopted by the group but not approved by the Charity Commissioners may help the group to run more smoothly but does not give it charitable status.

11 Groups which do not have charitable status should raise funds only from amongst the members of the group unless they have had specific exemption from the Inland Revenue.

12 Groups which need help in adopting the PPA constitution, working within the constitution of another organisation or devising their own set of rules should ask their local PPA branch for assistance.

13 Where there is an elected committee, this committee will be responsible for managing the resources, systems and equipment of the group. Although tasks may be delegated to individuals, the committee as a whole remains responsible.

14 Committee-run groups should hold an Annual General Meeting each year, following the procedure set out in their constitution or set of rules. Audited accounts should be presented to the membership and elections for the new committee, including the officers (Chair, Secretary and Treasurer), should take place.

15 Groups should at all times act within the framework of their constitution or set of rules. They should devote their resources solely to their accepted aims.

16 Groups which have adopted a charitable constitution and have income from investments (such as a deposit account at the bank) or own their premises or hold the leasehold must register as a charity. They should seek further advice from PPA to ensure that they are complying with other legal obligations.

17 Further information and advice about constitutions, charitable status and committee procedures can be found in PPA Information Sheets, PPA publications and from the PPA network.

18 Groups which are run just by an individual or as a partnership, and where money changes hands, should seek advice from the PPA National Centre since there may be further legal implications.

19 Groups should help parents take responsibility for management. They could:
- ensure meetings are held at mutually agreed times
- arrange for extra volunteers or staff to be on hand to ensure the safety of the children if meetings are held during the session
- give financial help and/or assist with arrangements for babysitting

- help arrange lifts or pay transport costs
- repay any out of pocket expenses promptly
- give clear information about what sort of involvement is needed and the amount of time and commitment it is likely to take.

20. Groups should ensure that all records and financial accounts are correct and kept up to date, subscriptions and insurance are paid and notes of decisions made at committee meetings and general meetings are recorded.

21. Groups which open a bank or building society account should ensure that two signatures are required on cheques or before money can be withdrawn. Two members of the group should receive copies of the monthly statement direct from the bank.

22. Groups should discuss their policy on behaviour and discipline. Any rules which they feel are necessary to maintain the safety and smooth running of the group should be written down and communicated clearly to all adults who attend.

23. Groups which encounter difficulties in resolving problems about behaviour and discipline should consult their PPA branch, local health visitor or social services adviser. Exclusion of any adult or child from the group should be used only as a very last resort.

24. All adults should be aware that they must not smack another person's child.

25. Any adult who is concerned about the physical or emotional welfare of a child in the group should contact the local social services department or the NSPCC.

EQUAL OPPORTUNITIES CONSIDERATIONS

i   Groups should develop, implement and monitor an equal opportunities policy.

ii Groups should try to ensure that their management committee is open and welcoming to all parents. They should take positive account of the various class, status, race, sex, age, cultural or religious backgrounds that make up our communities. Access should be provided for people with disabilities and interpreters for parents whose first language is not English.

SAFETY CONSIDERATIONS

i   Any child who is hurt during the session should be re-united as soon as possible with his/her parent. If first aid is necessary the parent should be consulted about any treatment.

ii Groups should review their safety, first aid and emergency procedures regularly and ensure that all adults are aware of these procedures. Further details about first aid, fire drills, incubation and exclusion periods for infectious diseases and common infections can be found in the Appendix.

iii German Measles (Rubella) is particularly dangerous to unborn babies so parents should not knowingly bring infected children to the group. Groups should inform parents when cases of German Measles have been identified so that women who may be pregnant can take appropriate action.

DOCUMENTS FOR PARENT AND TODDLER PLAYGROUPS

The documents and information acquired in the course of setting up and running a group should be kept in a safe place and be available for easy reference.

Those responsible for running the group need to know what the documents contain. When new people take over, the documents should be passed on and the purpose of each explained.

General documents

- Minutes of committee meetings and of general meetings
- List of members, including names of committee etc
- Set of rules for the group or a signed and dated constitution
- Copy of the group's welcome letter or leaflet
- Policy statements, eg equal opportunities policy, emergency procedures, rules about safety, behaviour and discipline
- Insurance policy or cover note (If the group employs staff, a copy of the certificate of employers' liability insurance must be displayed on the premises.)
- Equipment inventory, including details of any items on loan
- Account books showing income, expenditure and petty cash
- Bank/building society account details, including up to date list of signatures
- License/tenancy agreement or letter of agreement with landlord of lease
- Certificate of charitable status and charity number (if registered).

PPA membership details

- Membership number and membership card together with the member's information pack
- List of branch committee members, branch fieldworkers and area organisers
- List of county officers and county organiser
- PPA regional office address and telephone number
- PPA National Centre address and telephone number

Employment details

Any group employing staff should keep a separate folder for each employee which should contain:

- The job description and person specification
- Contracts of employment including disciplinary and grievance procedure and any other relevant details of terms and conditions of employment
- Records of any management meetings
- Inland Revenue/DSS information ie PAYE details and National Insurance number.

PLANNING THE SESSION

The session should be organised to meet the needs of both adults and children

in order to

make the group enjoyable for adults and stimulating for the children.

1 Groups should consider the needs of both adults and children when planning their session, although the emphasis may vary depending on the parents attending and the ages of the children.

2 PPA recognises that there is a variety of reasons why parents come to the group, such as to
● escape from the house
● meet people and make friends
● share some of the stresses, worries – and joys – of parenthood.
● seek opportunities for their children to play and to socialise.
Often they come for a mixture of these reasons.
Groups should consider these factors when planning their sessions.

3 The range of toys and equipment should take into account the ages and stages of development of the children.

4 All groups should have a basic range of toys and play materials suitable for babies, crawlers and toddlers, such as: rattles; soft toys; toys which can be explored with fingers or mouths; toys to push, pull, post, sort and build.

5 Groups should consider whether they wish to extend the range of play opportunities further by providing other toys and equipment suitable for toddlers and older pre-school children and/or arranging 'messy play' activities.
They may decide to provide a different activity, such as painting, glueing, dough or sand, each week or to organise several activities each session.

6 Before introducing these activities, groups should ensure that parents are generally in favour of them, since their success often depends upon the parents' co-operation and involvement with the children.

7 Parents should be encouraged to dress their children in 'play clothes' and protective aprons or overalls should be provided. Adults, too, may need reminding when messy activities are to take place so they can dress accordingly.

8 The adults responsible for the group should have regular meetings to plan and review the activities and the layout of the room and to consider the needs of the parents and children who attend.

9 During the session, children should be encouraged to select their own activities from the range provided. Where this includes 'messy play' or equipment such as a climbing frame, parents will need to stay close to their children, unless other adults are supervising the activity.

10 Adult seating should be provided, particularly by the baby area and any messy play activities, to encourage parents to accompany their children. Children should always have easy access to their parents.

11 Most groups rely upon as many parents as possible lending a hand before, during and after a session. Parents should be made aware that it is 'their group', that their help is needed and that anything they can do for the group is welcomed.

12 An explanation that 'no-one is paid, but we all work together as a team' often needs to be given. Even where there is a paid worker, parents should be aware that one person cannot run the group single handed.

13 Groups should consider how they can most successfully encourage parents to play a part in the day to day running of the group. They could
- ask parents to do relatively small jobs to begin with (unless they are keen to do more)
- give clear explanations about what needs doing
- get them to work with someone who knows what to do
- make sure the necessary equipment is provided (eg have a dustpan & brush ready by the sand)

- match the person with the job (Someone with a school age child may be able to arrive early, or make the drinks, but not stay late to clear up.)
- label boxes and shelves to enable easy identification of storage places
- clarify that it will not cost any money – and reimburse promptly for money spent eg on refreshments or equipment.
- try to share the jobs around, so everyone feels it is fair.
- regard things like 'talking to newcomers' as important contributions to running the group. That way a parent who cannot leave a baby or toddler to do a job will still be helping.
- listen to people's ideas and encourage them to ty out new things.
- thank parents for whatever contribution they make, however small.

14 Groups should recognise and accept that there are times when individual parents may not feel able to take on an active role. Groups should encourage parents to contribute only when the time seems appropriate.

15 Groups should consider the financial circumstances of the parents who come to the group. The entrance fee and any extra charges for refreshments should be set at a reasonable level. Groups should try to obtain funding or resources so that no parent is unable to attend through lack of money.

16 Groups trying to raise funds should not put undue pressure on parents to purchase items from clothes or book parties, buy raffle tickets, or make other extra financial contributions to the group.

EQUAL OPPORTUNITIES CONSIDERATIONS

i Activities reflecting the various aspects of our multi-cultural society should be integrated into all aspects of play especially the home corner, music and food preparation.

ii Books, pictures, posters, jigsaws, dolls, stories, rhymes and puzzles should be selected to show positive images of people of all races and cultures and to avoid racial or sexist stereotyping.

iii Consideration should be given to the personal and religious/cultural beliefs of parents if arrangements are made to celebrate festivals or birthdays. All cultures, religions and customs should be valued equally.

iv Adults with disabilities or learning difficulties should be encouraged to identify ways in which they would like to be involved in the group. Groups should make efforts to enable these contributions to be made.

SAFETY CONSIDERATIONS

i Although parents remain responsible for their own children, every adult within the group should be safety conscious; everyone should be encouraged to prevent accidents and remove any hazards.

ii Planning should ensure that the way activities are placed in relation to one another does not lead to added safety risks.

iii No-one should be asked to do jobs which are hazardous to themselves or their children. Making hot drinks with a baby under one arm or climbing on unstable furniture to stack equipment on high shelves, with or without a toddler in tow, should not be allowed.

iv A special area may need to be set aside for babies, to protect them from the activities of older children. This should have an easily washable floor covering.

PLAY ACTIVITIES AND EQUIPMENT

Groups should provide good quality, safe, educational play, with equipment and activities appropriate to the children's ages and stages of development

in order to

enable children to enjoy developing to their full potential.

[1]   Play is essential to children as the medium through which they learn and develop.

[2]   Groups should take into account the stages of children's development and include an appropriate selection of play activities.

[3]   **Small babies**
FOR THE FIRST FEW WEEKS OF LIFE, BABIES PRIMARILY NEED CARING ADULTS TO CUDDLE AND HOLD THEM, FRIENDLY FACES TO LOOK AT, VOICES TO LISTEN TO. From birth, babies learn through their senses about themselves and the world around them. As babies become more aware of their surroundings, adults need to ensure that the environment is sufficiently stimulating.

Groups could provide things to:
- look at   Posters, mobiles, toys and household objects with different shapes, colours and patterns, mirrors, shiny and dull objects, things that move.
- listen to   Singing, rhymes and music.
                   Bells, rattles, musical mobiles and toys.
- touch   Toys, fabrics and objects with different textures, shapes and weights.

[4]   **Older babies**
From about three months of age, when babies become more active, they also need opportunities to strengthen their muscles and increase control over eyes, head, hands and feet.

Groups (or parents) could provide things to:

● reach for or kick   Soft balls or toys (perhaps with a bell or rattle), paper or inflatable toys (including armbands) suspended across pram, mattress or bouncing chair.

● stimulate reach   toys which rock, roll or squeak when touched,
and grasp   rattles, soft toys, teethers, household objects (eg wooden spoons, plastic bowls), 'cot gym'.

Babies at this stage are likely to put everything they get hold of into their mouths. For reasons of safety and hygiene, some parents may prefer to provide playthings such as teethers and soft toys for their own babies rather than using communal toys.

5 Crawlers

Most babies become mobile, through crawling, rolling or bottom shuffling, between the ages of six and nine months. They need space to explore and try out their new skills, with a familiar adult close by. They continue to learn through their senses, so colour, shape, sound and texture are still important. Toys must be kept clean, though not necessarily sterile. All objects must be safe to chew since babies will put most things into their mouths.

Groups could provide things to:

● manipulate   activity centres and mats, buckets, boxes and baskets to fill and empty, household and natural objects, bricks to build and knock down, simple posting boxes, pop-up toys, stacking rings, toys with parts which move, soft balls and cubes, cars to push about, toy animals.

● make sounds   shakers, lids and spoons to bang, humming tops, bells, squeakers.

● encourage crawling balls, cylinders, plastic bottles, cars and other
and movement   toys which roll.

● look at   colourful plastic or cardboard books and/or catalogues showing everyday objects; an adult to share them with.

6 Just walking

When children are first beginning to walk, they need space to move in without getting knocked over and large equipment which will help them gain their balance. Anything they might pull themselves up on needs to be stable.

Groups could provide things to:

● push and pull   babywalkers to push (heavy ones, with a low centre of gravity to avoid tipping over), push-along toys such as prams, animals and toy machines, cardboard boxes to push or (with cord) to pull, other pull-along toys.

SIT-IN BABYWALKERS CAN BE HAZARDOUS.

7 | **Toddlers and Pre-School Children**

From 18 months or so, children enjoy a very wide range of play experiences, which can extend their development in many ways. Some particularly valuable activities – including most kinds of 'messy play' – require extra preparation and adult supervision, so groups which include these activities should plan them carefully.

Groups could provide opportunities for:

● Creative play   Scribbling and drawing with thick wax crayons, chalks or soft pencils
Painting, using thick brushes and non-toxic paint in non-spill pots and large sheets of paper at a table or low easel
Finger painting, sponge printing and other painting activities
Collage and junk modelling, using non-toxic glue with spatulas or brushes, glue pots and a wide variety of materials, cardboard boxes and scraps of every kind.

● Imaginative play   Dressing-up clothes such as hats, bags and shawls;
simple kitchen and household utensils (tea set, cutlery, pots & pans etc) from a variety of cultures;
dolls, garage and/or road mat and cars, toy animals, telephone, soft toys, hand and finger puppets;
screen for 'home corner', cooker, sink etc;
dough plus rollers, cutters, patty tins etc;
large shatterproof mirror;
simple train set.

● Story-telling   Bright attractive picture books; stories about familiar events and situations, including positive images of children and adults from a variety of races and cultures;

	book-corner with book-case and comfortable seating.
● Play with natural materials	Dough – large quantity of home-made dough, with different colours and varying recipes to give new experiences.
	Sand – washed silver sand in a baby bath, sand tray, or washing-up bowl; assortment of scoops, spades, buckets, rakes, plastic vehicles etc; moulds for wet sand; funnels and sieves for dry sand.
	Water – baby bath, water tray or washing up bowl; assortment of plastic containers, jugs; towels, waterproof aprons and floor covering.
	Clay, wood, peat etc.
● Making music and sounds	variety of simple instruments to shake, bang, scrape or pluck; rhymes, finger plays and songs.
● Physical play	toddler-size slide, large cardboard boxes, rocking horse or rocking chair, hidey box, plank, sit-and-ride toys (if there is a safe area to use them); simple climbing frame with cushioning floor mats or safety surfacing, play barrel, small stairs.
● Manipulative play, sorting, grading etc	interlocking bricks, blocks and shapes, lacing and threading sets, large peg boards and pegs, inset trays, shape-sorters, posting-boxes, stacking, fitting and nesting toys, toys to screw and turn, simple jigsaws.

8   Caring, interested adults can extend these play opportunities throughout the child's development. Adults are the small baby's first – and probably most important – plaything; the source of security from which the child can venture off to explore. They can encourage and stimulate, explain and interpret so that children can fully benefit from 'learning through play'.

9   Groups which are the main or only pre-school experience for children over three should consult PPA's *Good Practice for Sessional Playgroups* for further guidance on meeting the developmental needs of three to five year olds.

10   Children of all ages need creative experiences, with time to experiment,

to use materials in new ways, to explore possibilities and to take pleasure in the doing rather than the end product. No-one should be under any illusion that tasks such as copying and the collective or individual making of identical objects are creative activities.

[11] Protective clothing – eg aprons, sleeve guards, hats for sand – should be made available as necessary. Extra floor covering should be provided for messy activities and cleaning materials – eg dustpan and brush, mop and buckets, towels, bowls – should be easily accessible to adults.

[12] Groups should provide sufficient play materials so that wherever possible children can play alongside one another rather than having to be rivals for limited resources.

EQUAL OPPORTUNITIES CONSIDERATIONS

i   All groups, regardless of locality, should provide play activities and a range of equipment which reflect a variety of races and cultures. These should not be racist or sexist in nature or content.

SAFETY CONSIDERATIONS

i   Groups should choose sturdy, well made toys and play equipment constructed from non-toxic materials. Their design, including their size, should be appropriate to the ages of the children in the group.

ii   All toys should be of sufficient size and strength to prevent pieces being swallowed if they are chewed.

iii   Groups should look for the Lion Mark (British Toy Manufacturers' quality and safety symbol), the CE mark (the European Safety Symbol), and other recognised safety markings.

iv   Groups should ensure that any home-made toys are safe and well constructed.

v   All toys should be washed or sterilised regularly. Broken, damaged or unsuitable toys should be removed immediately.

vi   All other relevant safety and hygiene precautions should be taken; eg

---

climbing frames must be erected properly, dough changed frequently, outdoor sandpits covered, sand sieved and washed, dressing-up clothes and hats cleaned regularly.

vii   Groups should ensure that babies and crawlers are not harmed or over-restricted by play activities and equipment which are provided for older children.

viii Groups which share equipment with a playgroup should beware of borrowing unsuitable items, such as tall climbing frames or small construction bricks, beads or pegs.

ix   **Children should be adequately supervised at all times.** Some hazardous activities, such as water play, should be provided only if parents or other responsible adults ensure constant supervision.

CATERING ARRANGEMENTS

Groups should ensure that any food or drink provided is prepared hygienically and served safely and is appropriate to the needs of adults and children

in order to

extend the hospitality of the group to all families, avoid accidents and take account of specific dietary needs.

1. Most groups choose to provide refreshments for both adults and children. Hot or cold drinks for adults, cold drinks for children and a small snack are normally sufficient.

2. Groups should avoid food with a high salt, sugar or fat content and minimise the use of food or drink containing additives, preservatives or colouring.

3. Parent and toddler playgroups are not entitled to free milk, unlike sessional and full daycare playgroups.

4. In family drop-in centres where parents may be able to prepare their own meals, consideration should be given to the maintenance of safety and hygiene, and the nutritional value of the food.

5. Groups should decide upon the safest and most suitable way to organise their refreshments; extra help, from volunteers or staff, can be invaluable invaluable for preparing drinks and washing up; some groups will offer refreshments throughout the session, whereas others will have a specific time for serving refreshments.

6. Children and adults should be encouraged to sit down with their drinks.

7. Groups should ensure that suitable chairs are available for mothers who

wish to breast-feed their babies during the session.

8 Parents should be responsible for providing feeding bottles and preparing feeds for their own babies where these are required.

EQUAL OPPORTUNITIES CONSIDERATIONS

i Parents should be encouraged to suggest or provide alternatives for any food or drink which is considered inappropriate on medical, cultural or religious grounds.

ii A variety of food reflecting our multi-cultural society should be encouraged. Providing food from different countries and cultures not only gives positive recognition to families from those cultures but also encourages children to learn, enjoy and respect other traditions and cultures.

iii Groups should ensure that cooking utensils are used appropriately and sensitively according to dietary, religious and cultural requirements. Eg specific utensils should be reserved for Halal or Kosher food; a spoon used to dish up meat, fish fingers etc should not then be used to serve vegetarian food.

SAFETY CONSIDERATIONS

i Children should not be allowed unsupervised in the kitchen or other food preparation areas. Wherever possible they should be excluded from the kitchen altogether, particularly when hot drinks are being prepared.

ii Drinks such as tea or coffee made with boiling water can still scald after half an hour. Adults should ensure that all such drinks are placed out of reach of children and are not left unattended.

iii Hot drinks should be carried individually, not on trays.

iv Flexes from kettles and other electrical equipment should not be left dangling.

---

v   Groups should ensure that general rules of hygiene are followed when food and drink are being stored, prepared and served. No food or drink should be reheated.

vi All areas, surfaces and equipment used to prepare or serve food should be kept clean and in good repair. Cracked or chipped china should not be used.

vii Tea towels should be kept scrupulously clean and washed after each session.

viii Mugs or other containers for drinks should be stable to prevent spillage. Any spills which do occur should be mopped up as soon as possible.

ix If feeder beakers are used, these should be cleaned and sterilised regularly. Groups may prefer to ask parents to provide their own.

x   Great care should be taken if smoking is allowed. (See section on *Premises*). Lighted cigarettes should be kept well away from children's eye-level.

INSURANCE

Groups should have appropriate and adequate insurance cover

in order to

comply with statutory insurance responsibilities, protect the group's property and equipment, protect the group in the event of a valid claim against them and cover the children and adults in case of accident.

[1] All groups are strongly recommended to take out full insurance cover.

[2] Groups who pay staff – even if this is only £1 a week – have a statutory responsibility to take out Employers' Liability Insurance.

[3] Suggested Insurance Schemes cover:

a) Employments' Liability Insurance. Under the Employers' Liability (Compulsory Insurance) Act 1969 anyone who employs staff has a legal duty to insure against claims by workers for injury or disease. This insurance certificate must be displayed in the workplace. Volunteer helpers are also covered under this section in the PPA/Sun Alliance policy.

b) Public Liability Insurance. This covers legal liability for omissions or acts which cause injury or disease to third parties or loss or damage to their property. Third parties include group children, parents, visitors and all others with whom the group comes into contact. PPA recommends that all groups should take out Public Liability Insurance to protect individuals involved from personal costs should legal action for liability be successful.

Even though parents in parent and toddler playgroups officially remain responsible for their own children, there are many circumstances in which the group, or the person deemed to be the group leader, could be held responsible in law.

c) Personal Accident Insurance. This may provide some limited compensation for injury where no negligence is involved.

d) Equipment and Contents Insurance against theft, fire, flood etc.

e) Money and personal effects.

Extra cover can also be obtained for vehicles, buildings (if owned by the group) and accidental damage to electrical and mechanical equipment.

4 PPA in conjunction with Sun Alliance has full Insurance Schemes to cover the above.

a) Many parent and toddler playgroups which are attached to or use the same premises as a playgroup are eligible to insure through that playgroup.

b) Most PPA branches – and counties where there is no branch – operate the PPA/Sun Alliance branch umbrella scheme which provides full insurance cover at a reduced rate for small parent and toddler playgroups. Groups should contact their local PPA branch or PPA county to see if they are eligible to use this scheme.

c) If neither of the above options is possible, and particularly for large groups which cannot use the branch umbrella scheme, insurance can be obtained by becoming group members of PPA and insuring directly with National PPA.

Insurance information and advice can be obtained from the PPA Group Insurance Prospectus and the Insurance Officer at PPA National Centre.

5 An inventory of equipment, furniture etc must be kept and updated regularly for insurance purposes. Loss or damage by authorised users, theft and malicious damage may be covered differently on some policies and groups should check their own policy carefully.

6 Before taking children on outings, groups should ensure that drivers have appropriate vehicle insurance. Drivers should check with their insurance company concerning the number of children their insurance covers.

7 Groups should have clear procedures for the reporting of incidents and dealing with claims.

8 Accidents involving equipment may lead to a claim on a public liability and/or manufacturer's products liability insurance. Groups should check that the maker of home-made equipment has liability cover or their group's members might be unable to claim realistic damages.

9 Groups are sometimes told that they are covered by the insurance held by the owners of the building. They should always ask for a copy of the

policy and check their position.

10 Groups which meet in different members' homes each week can insure under options 3(b) or (c) as above. In the event of a claim being made against them, some members may be covered under their Household Insurance Policy but it is quite likely that not all members would have suitable insurance cover.

11 Groups should be aware of the personal and financial consequences of inadequate insurance policies. Without insurance any liability claim would be against the person seen in law as being responsible for the accident. That person would have to pay damages from her/his own resources.

EQUAL OPPORTUNITIES CONSIDERATIONS

i All children and adults including those with disabilities are covered by the group's public liability insurance. Claims for accidental bodily injury to an adult or child with disabilities may not be met under the personal accident section as this can exclude any injury caused or contributed to by any "pre-existing physical or mental health defect". This clause is standard in these policies.

EMPLOYING STAFF

All groups should pay realistic expenses to volunteers; groups employing staff should comply with all employment legislation and pay adequate salaries

in order to

enable volunteers to take part in the group, recognise the responsible and skilled nature of work with children and parents and protect the rights of employees.

1   Groups should provide realistic expenses for volunteers. They should ensure that all costs are adequately covered and out of pocket expenses are repaid promptly.

2   Groups which employ staff, even if they just pay someone £1 a week, must ensure that they are aware of and comply with legislation covering employees' statutory rights, tax and insurance, including operating the PAYE system.

3   Groups which employ staff, or are considering doing so, should refer to the Appendix for further information about employment.

4   Groups should ensure that they have clear management procedures before employing any staff. Employees need to know to whom they are accountable; in most cases this would be to an elected management committee. Groups where no-one has clear responsibility for the group are advised not to employ staff.

5   Under-fives playgroups, where some of the children are cared for in the absence of their parents, must also adhere to all local authority regulations regarding the employment of staff, including health declarations and disclosure of criminal convictions.

6   No such regulations apply to groups which are not required to register with the local social services department, although some members of staff may already have undergone checks because of their work in

playgroups or as child-minders. Groups should consider, and, where necessary, discuss with their PPA branch or local social services department how prospective staff or volunteers coming into the group can be adequately vetted.

7 Working with young children and their families is highly responsible, emotionally demanding and physically taxing. Wherever possible salary levels for staff in groups should reflect this and be comparable to those of others working in local sessional pre-school services.

8 Any group considering appointing staff can seek advice on drawing up job descriptions and person specifications, and get help in interviewing, from their local PPA branch. Representatives from the management committee or other parents from the group should be involved in, and have responsibility for, the recruitment and selection of staff.

9 Unsuccessful applicants should have the right to discuss their interview and know the reasons for their non-appointment.

10 There should be a probationary period and a planned induction programme for all new employees so that they have a clear understanding of their role within the group.

EQUAL OPPORTUNITIES CONSIDERATIONS

i Groups which employ staff should draw up a clear Equal Opportunities policy to cover recruitment and selection procedures, job descriptions, person specifications, accountability, support, expenses and training opportunities. Further help and advice is available from PPA National Centre.

ii Groups employing staff or recruiting volunteers should aim to reflect the ethnicity of the local community and to have adults present in the group who can speak the first language of the families in the area.

iii Advertising for staff should not be done just by word of mouth.

VOLUNTEERS AND STAFF: SKILLS, ATTITUDES AND TRAINING

Volunteers and staff in groups need to develop attitudes and skills which promote the self-esteem and well-being of both adults and children

in order to

encourage the development of self-confidence which enables adults and children to reach their full potential.

1 Parents responsible for running groups, together with any other volunteers and staff, should be aware that other parents will often look to them for example and advice; the way they interact with and respond to the children is likely to be taken as a model by other parents.

2 The adults should work as a team for the benefit of the group. They should demonstrate that they are happy to work together by the exchange of comments, information, looks and smiles. They should show care and respect for each other and all members of the group.

3 The adults responsible for the group should help parents develop self-esteem by:
- getting to know each parent as an individual
- calling parents by name (not just "Saroj's mum", "Nicky's childminder")
- consulting with parents about all aspects of running the group
- using the parents' skills and expertise, and valuing whatever contribution they make to the group
- being non-judgemental about the parents' methods of child-rearing, but still encouraging good practice.

4 Adults should listen and talk to children in a positive way and respect them as unique individuals. They should use children's names when talking to them and show their interest by getting down to the children's

level, maintaining eye contact, and in their general manner.

5   Adults should be especially responsive to children who are distressed. They should reunite children with their parents for further comfort and reassurance.

6   Adults should assist children to acquire new skills and concepts by providing new experiences and encouraging children's natural curiosity.

7   Children may need help in acquiring techniques, such as holding a crayon or dressing a doll. Adults should intervene in a sensitive way, at times appropriate to the child, to enable children to learn according to their needs.

8   PPA recognises the prime importance of the development of children's language. Volunteers and staff in groups can encourage children's use of language both by their direct interaction with children and by the example they give to parents. They should:
● take time to listen and respond
● talk to babies and reply to their babble
● talk to children about what they see and events that are happening
● help children name objects/sounds etc
● ask open ended questions
● encourage children to talk about their feelings.

9   Adults should recognise the value to children's language development of a singing or rhyme session, particularly one where the parent participates with the baby or toddler.

10   Although parents are responsible for managing the behaviour of their own children, other adults can demonstrate suitable ways to develop self-discipline and respect for the needs of others. Volunteers and staff should use only positive methods of guidance for children, such as:
● redirection
● anticipation and removal of potential problems
● positive reinforcement and encouragement.
They should avoid competition, unnecessary comparison and direct criticism. They should never use corporal punishment or other humiliating and frightening punishment methods.

11 Adults should encourage children to develop socially and praise them when they co-operate, take turns and help each other and adults.

12 All interaction with children should take account of their age and stage of development, and their ability to understand. Verbal instructions could be complemented by
- gestures eg pointing
- miming the required task
- physical help eg taking the hand.

13 All adults who are involved in or responsible for running groups should have access to PPA training.

14 Volunteers and staff who spend time in the group on a more permanent basis should be strongly encouraged to undergo training. They should aim to develop skills, attitudes, expertise and understanding of the needs of adults and children.

15 PPA believes adult learning is a continuous process. PPA recognises and values the experience of parenting and home management as a basis for further development through training.

16 PPA training is available in a variety of forms and is a shared experience. Fuller details are available in PPA's publication, *Adults Learning in PPA – A Training Guide.*

17 The costs of training should be included in the group's budget.

18 PPA is actively involved in the development of National Vocational Qualifications (NVQ) and believes this will be the way for parents and carers to validate their skills and experience and to progress, if they wish, within a training framework.

EQUAL OPPORTUNITIES CONSIDERATIONS

i   Children may need to be encouraged to be non-sexist in their choice of activities.

ii   Racist and sexist attitudes or remarks should be challenged and discussed sensitively. Care should be taken to deal with the behaviour and not seem to be attacking the speaker personally. Children or adults suffering this type of abuse should be supported and comforted if necessary.

iii   Groups should recognise the importance of children's first language or dialect as their primary means of expression. Parents should be encouraged to use this first language with their children.

iv   Children who have English as a second language should have verbal instructions complemented by gestures, miming and physical help as necessary.

v   Children and adults should not be made to feel inadequate because of their lack of competence in language especially if they are learning a second language or have a learning difficulty or a disability which affects their speech. Likewise adults should not be made to feel inadequate because of any lack of educational achievement.

vi   Training events should be held in fully accessible premises whenever possible.

vii   Signers, interpreters and help for the visually impaired should be provided at training events when necessary.

SAFETY CONSIDERATIONS

i   Safe facilities should be provided for children who accompany adults on training events.

LINKS WITH LOCAL PROVISION

Groups should maintain close links with other local provision and services for under-fives and their families

in order to

provide continuity for the children's development and continuing support for families.

[1] Groups should be in regular contact with the local PPA network. Groups should be invited to attend PPA branch meetings as well as any special events held for parent and toddler playgroups.

[2] Groups should inform their PPA branch as soon as possible of any changes of address and ensure that details about the group are kept up to date.

[3] Regular contact should be maintained with health visitors and early education and social services advisers. Some groups may wish to encourage health visitors to hold regular baby clinics within the group.

[4] Groups should liaise with the local National Childbirth Trust (NCT) and any other provision for mothers and babies in the area, so that parents from these organisations will find it easier to join the group.

[5] Groups should maintain close links with local sessional or full daycare playgroups and nursery schools. They should have information for parents available about provision for under-fives in the area and be ready to advise parents on what to look for in a playgroup. Playleaders from local playgroups could be invited along to the group to meet parents and children.

[6] A parent and toddler playgroup which uses the same premises as a sessional playgroup should investigate whether it would be beneficial for the groups to be run by one committee, hold fundraising events

together and/or share some of their equipment.

7 Groups should consider developing links with local religious or cultural groups and other community providers where appropriate.

8 Schools and colleges may ask if their students can attend the group or make contact with parents through it. Groups which agree to provide such training placements for teenagers and young people should insist that they receive full details of what is expected from them and ensure close liaison is maintained. Guidance can be found in PPA's booklet, *Teenagers in Playgroups* and from the local PPA branch or county association.

9 Groups should be represented on the management or users' committee of premises they share or rent from another organisation and play as full a part as possible in its activities.

Appendix 1

1. Parents remain responsible for their own children at the group and should always be on the premises. In the event of an accident involving a child, the parent will therefore normally be responsible for reassuring the child and administering first aid or agreeing to it being administered by another person.

2. If the parent is extremely distressed, it may be necessary for another person to take temporary charge of the situation. The parent should be reassured, comforted and consulted about any treatment.

3. If the sick/injured child has been brought to the group by a childminder or other adult carer, the child's parent should be contacted as soon as possible. However, if the sickness/injury is severe, the group should not wait for the parent to come but should summon a doctor or ambulance immediately.

4. Groups should identify which of their members have first aid training so they can be called upon in an emergency. Members of the group could be encouraged to undertake first aid training so that someone who is trained in first aid is present at each session.

5. Groups are advised to appoint a named person to take charge of any accidents (eg to call an ambulance, administer first aid etc). All adults who attend the group regularly should be aware who this person is.

6. A named person should be responsible for the first aid box which should always be refilled after use. All adults should be aware of its location.

7. In the event of an accident, adults in the group should keep calm, reassure those who have witnessed the accident and remove any remaining hazards (such as broken toys) in order to prevent further injury.

8. If a parent is injured or taken ill, the group should make suitable

arrangements for her/his child/ren whilst first aid or medical treatment is being given.

9   **An accident book** should be kept readily available on the premises for the recording of all accidents to adults and children, however slight. Minor injuries can give rise to more serious symptoms later and accurate details could be vital. Particulars should be recorded as soon as the incident has been dealt with, whilst details are still clearly remembered.

10 *Details to be recorded are: the full name of the casualty; date, time and place of accident; circumstances in which it occurred; nature of injuries; treatment given and medical aid sought; names of witnesses and person dealing with the accident.* If the accident is to a child then the parent/carer (who should normally have been present throughout any treatment) should also sign the relevant entry in the Accident Book.

11 The book should be inspected periodically by the committee or other adults responsible for running the group. This may help pinpoint hazards and danger areas which need looking at and could prevent further accidents. The accident book should be kept indefinitely.

12 Groups should always send details of any serious accident or head injury to the insurance company (PPA's Insurance Officer if covered by the PPA/Sun Alliance scheme) in case the accident gives rise to a claim some years later.

13 It is recommended that surgical or other waterproof gloves should be used when dealing with sickness/injuries involving body fluids and that a mask should be used when giving expired air resuscitation.

14 Groups which employ staff should be aware that all employers are liable for the health and safety of their employees under the Health and Safety Act 1974 and Health and Safety (First Aid) Regulations 1981.

Appendix 2

This should be a strong container, impervious to dust and damp, clearly labelled with a white cross on a green background.

The following contents are recommended by the Health and Safety Executive, amounts varying with numbers involved:

ITEM	NUMBERS IN GROUP 1-5	6-10	11-50
Guidance card	1	1	1
Individually wrapped sterile adhesive dressings	10	20	40
Sterile eye-pads with attachment	1	2	4
Triangular bandages	1	2	4
Sterile coverings for serious wounds	1	2	4
Safety pins	6	6	12
Medium size sterile unmedicated dressings	3	6	8
Large sterile unmedicated dressings	1	2	4
Extra large sterile unmedicated dressings	1	2	4

Where children are being cared for other items needed could be:

A pair of sharp scissors

A pair of tweezers

A roll of non-allergic adhesive tape (micropore)

Packs of sterile gauze

Crepe bandage

Cotton wool

Finger stall

A container of boiled water

Surgical or other waterproof gloves to be worn when dealing with bleeding, vomiting and incontinence

Mask for wearing when giving expired air resuscitation.

It is useful to stock some items for adult use only, eg sanitary protection wear.

It may also be more appropriate to have recommended contents in differing quantities because of the number of children (eg more triangular bandages).

Whenever an item is used it must be replaced as soon as possible.

Other information and equipment which groups should have available for use in an emergency include:

● details of nearest accident and emergency unit

● phone card or money for pay-phone

● phone numbers of doctors, taxi firms, ambulance station (if women going into labour are expected to ring direct).

FIRST AID PROCEDURES

	SYMPTOMS	ACTION	NEVER
BREATHING STOPPED	Unconsciousness, blue lips and finger nails, no movement of chest wall, child is silent – no sound of breathing.	Clear the airway of debris or obstructions. Open the airway by extending the head. Give mouth to mouth (or mouth to nose) ventilation. Action in the first 3 minutes is vital.	NEVER. . . Panic or waste time.
HEART STOPPED	As above plus no carotid pulse felt.	Mouth to mouth ventilation plus external chest compression. This should only be attempted by people who are experienced with external cardiac compression.	NEVER. . . Panic or waste time.
SEVERE BLEEDING	May be obvious site of bleeding. Feeling faint, general weakness. Nausea, pallor, especially face. Thirst. Increase in pulse rate but weak.	Apply direct pressure on the wound using fingers and thumb, over a sterile dressing if possible. Use a ring pad if foreign body present. Lie the child down. Raise the injured part (unless you suspect a fracture). Apply sterile pad and bandage.	NEVER. . . leave the child alone or give drinks. Never apply a tourniquet.
UNCONSCIOUS	The child is lying silent. Does not respond to questions, may not respond to pain.	Check breathing. Try to establish the cause. Loosen tight clothing. If breathing turn the child to the recovery position unless fracture of spine suspected.	NEVER. . . give drinks or leave the child alone.
BURNS & SCALDS	Pain, usually with redness and swelling at the injury. Blisters later.	Immerse in cold water for at least 10 minutes. Cover with a dry sterile dressing and bandage. Any burn greater than 1cm square should be seen by a doctor. For large burns dial 999.	NEVER. . . apply butter or lard, cream or ointments. Never burst any blisters.
CHOKING	Caused by obstruction to airway, eg food. Violent coughing. Difficulty breathing. Congestion of face. Eventual unconsciousness.	Place the child over your knee, head down, slap between the shoulder blades up to 4 times. Check in mouth for dislodged foreign body. If unsuccessful, perform abdominal thrust up to 4 times.	
CONVULSIONS OR FITS	May be twitching of face and limbs, upward eyes, rigidity of body, frothing at mouth, breath holding, unconsciousness plus high temperature in children.	Make sure he can breathe, and that he does not injure himself by striking hard objects. Loosen constricting clothing. Make sure the child sees his doctor. Cool the child with tepid sponging if temperature high.	NEVER. . . lie the child flat on his back. Never leave the child alone. Never forcibly restrain the child.

62

Condition	Signs/Symptoms	What to do	NEVER
FALLS AND FRACTURES	Could range from bruising to fracture to unconsciousness.	If minor fall, tender loving care is best. If the bruising/swelling is extensive, ease with a cold compress. If you suspect a fracture, do not move the injured part unless absolutely necessary.	NEVER... move the child unnecessarily if you suspect a fracture.
HEAD INJURIES	May be loss of consciousness, nausea and vomiting, amnesia, bruising, bleeding. May be no obvious symptoms.	Lie the child down in the recovery position, keep him warm and calm. Get help immediately and move as little as possible. Keep under observation. Remember to tell a parent even if injury was only slight.	NEVER... rule out damage to the brain even if no signs or symptoms.
POISONING (household articles)	Range from stomach ache and vomiting to obvious burning of lips to unconsciousness.	Take the child, and the cause of the poison, to the hospital immediately. Check breathing. Begin resuscitation if breathing stops. Give child drink of water if lips burnt and child conscious.	NEVER... leave the child alone. Never make the child vomit.
EYES (foreign body)	Visible redness and watering of eye. Pain and itching.	Try to prevent child rubbing eye. Natural watering of eye will remove small pieces of sand. Continue by irrigating eye with cold water. Other foreign bodies need medical attention.	NEVER... leave an eye injury. If you are unhappy take the child to hospital.
EARS	Crying and holding ear. Perhaps foreign object sticking out of ear.	Earache. Contact a parent and advise that the child sees a doctor. Foreign body. Prevent child from touching ear. Foreign body needs to be removed in hospital.	NEVER... press on the object – you may damage the ear.
NOSE BLEED	Bleeding from the nose.	Sit the child down, head tilted forward, and pinch the end of his nostrils for 10 minutes. Try to prevent child blowing nose or picking it after bleeding stopped.	NEVER... lie the child on his back or put his head back.
BITES	Punctured skin or just teeth marks at the site of the injury.	Clean with soap and water and check with parents that the child is immunised against tetanus, if bitten by an animal.	NEVER... approach the animal if it is frothing at the mouth.
CUTS/GRAZES	Blood at the site of the injury.	Press gently at the site of the cut or graze. Clean with soap and water and cover with dry dressing or plaster.	NEVER... cover without cleaning.
STINGS	Swelling and redness where the child has been stung. Sting may still be present.	Swelling in the throat, on the tongue or near the eyes can be dangerous. Take to the hospital. If you can see the sting remove with tweezers.	NEVER... leave the child alone until the swelling disappears.
SPRAINS & STRAINS	Severe swelling and bruising which is painful.	Apply a cold compress. Support the injury with a pad and crepe bandage.	NEVER... bathe the injury in hot water.

Appendix 3

INCUBATION AND EXCLUSION PERIODS
OF THE COMMON INFECTIOUS DISEASES

Disease	Usual Incubation Period (Days)	Interval Between Onset of Illness and Appearance of Rash (Days)	Minimum Period of Exclusion Provided Child Appears Well	
			Patients	Family Contacts
CHICKEN POX	10-21	0-2	Seven days from appearance of rash: all the scabs need not have separated	There is no routine exclusion of contacts of any of these infectious diseases but individual children
DYSENTERY	1-7	–	Until 24 hours after cessation of diarrhoea	may be excluded on the advice of a General Medical Practitioner
FOOD POISONING	0-2	–	Until declared fit	
GERMAN MEASLES	14-21	0-2	Until clinical recovery	
INFECTIVE JAUNDICE	14-42	–	Until clinical recovery	
MEASLES	7-21	3-5	Until clinical recovery	
MENINGITIS	2-10	–	Until clinical recovery and bacteriological examination is clear	
MUMPS	12-28	–	Until disappearance of all swelling	
SCARLET FEVER	2-5	1-2	Until clinical recovery	
WHOOPING COUGH	5-14	–	Until clinical recovery	

Appendix 4

DISEASE	MINIMUM PERIOD OF EXCLUSION
IMPETIGO	Until spots have healed, unless lesions can be covered.
PEDICULOSIS (HEAD LICE)	Until treatment has been carried out successfully.
VERRUCAE (PLANTAR WARTS)	Exclusion from barefoot activities until certified free from infection.
RINGWORM OF FEET (ATHLETE'S FOOT)	Exclusion from barefoot activities until certified free from infection.
RINGWORM OF SCALP OR BODY	Until adequate treatment instituted, provided lesions are covered.
THREADWORM	Until adequate treatment instituted.
SCABIES	Until adequate treatment instituted.

If you need any further help or advice please contact your General Medical Practitioner or Local Health Clinic.

Small babies are particularly susceptible to other common infections such as coughs, colds, diarrhoea and sickness. Anyone suffering from these infections, including older children who are considered unfit for school, should be discouraged from coming to the group, especially when small babies are present.

Appendix 5

FIRE PREVENTION AND FIRE DRILLS

The Fire Officer must inspect the premises of any group, such as an under-fives group, which needs to register with the social services department. The group may then be given specific instructions with which it must comply before opening.

Premises for parent and toddler playgroups do not have to be inspected in this way. Groups should still seek advice from the Fire Officer on suitable maximum numbers, fire alarms, fire drill, fire extinguishers and other aspects of fire safety.

FIRE PREVENTION

[1] Check that all heaters are being used in accordance with the manufacturer's instructions.

[2] Check that any heating system is being maintained correctly.

[3] Check all plugs and leads regularly.

[4] Insist that smoking rules are observed on the premises.

[5] All soft furnishings should be made of flame-resistant material.

[6] All heaters should be well guarded and no paper or material should be near enough to catch fire.

[7] When in use, the cooker should never be left unattended.

[8] There should be free access to all doors and fire exits, which should be kept unlocked. Prams and pushchairs must not be left blocking exists.

[9] Fire extinguishers should be checked annually; the adults responsible for the group should know where they are and how to use them.

[10] Everyone should know the whereabouts of the nearest telephone. If use of a pay phone is necessary, coins or a phone card should be kept in an accessible place.

FIRE DRILL

[1] Groups should agree upon a fire safety policy. In many cases, particularly for large groups, this should include a regular fire drill to practise quick, safe evacuation of the building.

[2] Although it is important not to frighten the children, the adults responsible for the group need to feel confident that adults and children will respond immediately to fire drill instructions and leave the building in an orderly manner.

[3] Groups which do not currently hold fire drills should still ensure that all adults are aware of what to do in case of fire. A trial fire drill may well bring to light unforeseen difficulties in evacuating the premises and demonstrate that a regular fire drill would be advisable.

[4] The group will need its own fire alarm, which should be used exclusively for fire drill or in a genuine emergency. It should make a loud arresting sound and should be easily accessible during each session.
The Fire Service recommend a 12 cm bell.

[5] A daily attendance register, showing both adults and children, should be completed as families arrive and leave, so that a clear record of who is on the premises is always available.

[6] The fire drill procedure will need to be considered carefully by the group, taking into account the premises and the accesses available. Specific areas of responsibility – such as for checking the kitchen and toilets, collecting and checking the register and phoning for the emergency services – should be allocated to adults who attend the group regularly.

[7] Parents will normally be responsible for escorting their own child/ren off the premises and taking them to a pre-arranged assembly point. Before parents can take on other areas of responsibility they will need to be

certain that their own children are being safely looked after.

8   The assembly points identified in the fire drill should be at least 25 yards away from the building.

9   The fire drill procedure should be clearly displayed for all parents, visitors and helpers to see. Members of the committee or other adults responsible for the group should all be given a copy.

10   In order to be fully effective, and to take into account the irregular attendance at the group, fire drills need to be held frequently, perhaps as often as once every two months.

11   Groups which meet in people's homes should adapt these guidelines to their own situation. All adults should be told the position of the doors out of the house and ensure these doors are kept clear.

Appendix 6

[1] Groups which employ staff should comply with current employment legislation.

[2] All employees have statutory rights regardless of their length of service or level of earnings. These include the right:

- not to be discriminated against on grounds of race, sex or marriage
- to equal pay with members of the opposite sex doing similar work or work of a similar value
- to an itemised pay statement
- to a safe working environment in line with the requirements of the Safety at Work Act 1974 and subsequent regulations
- to reasonable time-off for public duties (this need not be paid)
- to paid time-off for ante-natal care
- to belong to a trade union and take part in its activities
- not to be unfairly dismissed for union activities.

[3] Any group paying someone more than £1 per week must operate the PAYE income tax system. Details of how to do this are given on the next page.

[4] Other statutory rights and duties are dependent upon the number of hours worked, the length of service and the level of earnings.

[5] Groups where employees work or have worked
- for 16 hours or more per week
- for 8 hours or more in the same group for 5 years or more
- for 8 hours or more in the same group where they have previously worked 16 hours per week for at least 2 years

will need to comply with the Employment Protection Act 1975 which further extends these statutory rights.

[6] If employees earn more than the lower earnings limit (£43 per week in 1989) then National Insurance Contributions will also need to be paid and

a Statutory Sickness Pay Scheme operated.

[7] If they need further information and advice, or if they are uncertain about whether any particular employment legislation applies to them, groups are recommended to contact the PPA National Centre, their local Inland Revenue Office or Department of Social Security.

[8] All figures and information quoted here are subject to change. Groups should ensure the information they use is up to date.

PAYE

The Income Tax position for staff members of your group

When employing staff, you may have to register with the local Tax Office. They will allocate your group a reference number and send you all the necessary forms, tables and notes. The people in the Tax Office are usually very helpful to new employers who have just started having to operate PAYE.
If you follow this procedure, your group will not be held responsible if an employee has failed to inform you about other income earned.

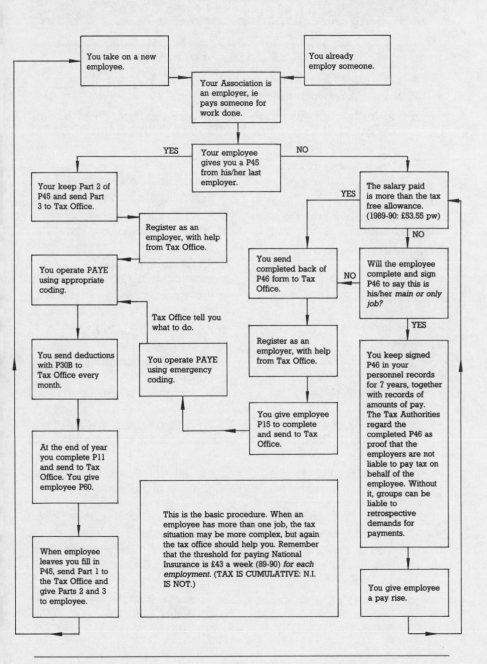

Appendix 7

[1] **PPA and Sister Organisations in the UK**

(a) **PPA Publications.** Full catalogue available from PPA National Centre, 61-63 Kings Cross Road, London WC1X 9LL. (Tel: 071 833 0991. Fax: 071 837 4942.

Publications include:

- Starting a Parent and Toddler Playgroup
- Play and Playthings in Mother and Toddler Groups
- Accident Prevention and First Aid
- Starting a PPA group
- "Let's Play" booklets:
  Let's Pretend
  Sounds and Music
  Junk Play
  Books and Storytelling
- Business Side of Playgroup
- Settling at Playgroup

- Playgroup Activities
- Wordplay, Fingerplay
- More Wordplay, Fingerplay
- PPA Group Constitution and notes
- All Children are Special . . . some need extra help
- PPA Account Book
- PPA Register
- Adults Learning in PPA (A Training Guide)
- You Can Help (a guide to the 1981 Education Act).
- Teenagers in Playgroups

A Resource List with details of PPA Information Sheets is available from PPA National Centre. Please enclose a stamped self-addressed envelope.

Other publications which are particularly relevant to parent and toddler playgroups are available from some PPA Regional Offices.

(b) **SPPA Publications** (Scotland PPA). List available from SPPA, 14 Elliot Place, Glasgow G3 8EP. (Tel: 041-221-4148)

(c) **NiPPA Publications** (Northern Ireland PPA). List available from NiPPA, 14 Wellington Park, Belfast, Northern Ireland BT9 6DJ. (Tel: 0232-662825)

(d) **Wales PPA Publications.** List available from Wales PPA, 2a, Chester Street, Wrexham, Clwyd, Wales LL13 8BD. (Tel: 0978-358195).

2 **Useful Organisations: Contact telephone numbers**

(a) General
- Child Poverty Action Group — 071-253-3406
- Commission for Racial Equality — 071-828-7022
- Crying Babies Support Group (CRYSIS) — 071-404-5011
- Equal Opportunities Commission — 061-8339244
- Family Centre Network — 071-833-3319
- Foundation for Study of Infant Deaths — 071-235-0965
- Gingerbread — 071-240-0953
- Home-Start Consultancy — 0533-554988
- National Association for Maternal and Child Welfare — 071-491-2772
- National Association for the Welfare
  of Children in Hospital (NAWCH) — 071-833-2041
- National Childbirth Trust (NCT) — 081-992-8637
- National Childminding Association (NCMA) — 081-464-6164
- National Council for One-Parent Families — 071-267-1361
- National Out of School Alliance (NOOSA) — 071-739-4787
- National Playbus Association — 0272-775375
- National Society for the Prevention of
  Cruelty to Children (NSPCC) — 071-242-1626
- National Stepfamily Association — 0223-460312
- Organisation for Parents Under Stress (OPUS) — 081-645-0469
- Parents Anonymous — 071-263-8918
- Play for Life — 0603-505947
- Play Matters (Toy Libraries Association) — 071-387-9592
- Relate (Marriage Guidance) — 0788-73241
- Stillbirth and Neonatal Death Society (SANDS) — 071-436-5881
- Terence Higgins Trust — 071-831-0330
- Twins and Multiple Birtsh Association — 0384-373642
- We Welcome Small Children National Campaign — 071-586-3453
- Working Group Against Racism in Children's Resources — 071-627-4594

b) For Children or Adults with Disabilities
- Association for All Speech Impaired Children (AFASIC) — 071-236-3632
- Association for SPina Bifida and Hydrocephalus — 071-388-1382
- Downs Syndrome Association — 071-720-0008
- Eczema Society — 071-388-4097
- National Association for Deaf-Blind and
  Rubella Handicapped (SENSE) — 071-278-1005
- National Deaf Children's Society — 071-229-9272
- Network 81 — 0279-503244
- Royal National Institute for the Blind (RNIB) — 071-388-1266
- Royal Society for Mentally Handicapped Children
  (MENCAP) — 071-253-9433

– Spastics Society   071-636-5020
– Voluntary Council for the Handicapped Child   071-278-9441

Many of these organisations have local contact numbers. Further information can be obtained from your local library, health visitor or social services department.

3   Selected Reading

Author	Title	Publisher	Year
Jane Asher	Keep Your Baby Safe	Penguin	1988
Bruno Bettelheim	A Good Enough Parent	Pan	1988
Tony Bradman	The Essential Father	Unwin	1985
Dorothy Butler	Babies Need Books	Penguin	1988
Commission for Racial Equality	From Cradle to School	CRE	1990
Edwina Conner	Pre-School Play Activities	Macdonald	1987
Brenda Crowe	Living with a Toddler	Unwin, Hyman	1982
Brenda Crowe	Play is a Feeling	Unwin, Hyman	1984
Brenda Crowe	Your Child and You	Unwin, Hyman	1986
David Crystal	Listen to Your Child	Penguin Revised	1989
Louise Derman-Sparkes	Anti Bias Curriculum	NAEYC (from VOLCUF)	1989
Joyce Donoghue	Running a Mother and Toddler Club	Unwin	1984
Dorothy Einon	Creative Play	Penguin	1986
Gee and Meredith	Entertaining and Educating Babies & Toddlers/Young Children	Usborne	1987
Jones & Pritchett	Understanding Child Abuse	Macmillan	1987
Penelope Leach	Baby and Child	Penguin Revised	1989
Penelope Leach	The Parents' A-Z	Penguin	1985
Elizabeth Matterson	Play with a Purpose for under 7s	Penguin New Ed	1989
Elizabeth Matterson	This Little Puffin	Puffin	1969
Maire Messenger Davies	Baby Language	Unwin, Hyman	1987
J & E Newson	Toys and Playthings	Penguin	1979
Open University	The First Years of Life	Ward Lock	1979
Open University	The Pre-School Child	Ward Lock	1979
Osborn and Milbank	The Effects of Early Education	Oxford UP	1987
Mary Sheridan	Spontaneous Play in Early Childhood	NFER/ Nelson Reprint	1985
Tizard and Hughes	Young Children Learning	Fontana	1984
Rhona Whiteford	Ready for School	Scholastic	1988